# Introduction

Communication is, without question, the most valuable skill any manager can possess. It is the link between ideas and action, the process that generates profit. Communication is the emotional glue that binds humans together in relationships, personal and professional. The ability to communicate is what connects people to others in an organization, an industry, or a society. To be skilled at it is to be at the heart of what makes enterprise, private or public, function successfully.

*Effective Communication* focuses on the processes involved in business communication and concentrates, in particular, on ways in which you can become more effective by becoming more knowledgeable and skilled as a communicator. All forms of communication, whether writing, listening, or speaking, are the end-products of a process that begins with critical thinking.

This book covers a wide range of topics designed to help you understand the communication process better, from planning a strategy to the analysis of your audience. It provides you with guidelines for preparing and delivering an effective speech, as well as ideas for expressing yourself on paper. There are tips for dealing with the specific challenges of team communication, including how to run a meeting, give feedback, and resolve conflict. Finally, it gives you ideas for communicating with clients and customers and thinking about your brand and identity. It's all here. The next step is up to you.

# Chapter 1

# Understanding communication skills

Communication is more than just a way to get ideas across or exchange points of view. It is the process by which we interact with others and seek out information essential to our daily lives, allowing us to control the circumstances in which we work.

# Defining communication

Think of communication as a process, involving senders and receivers who encode and decode messages that are transmitted by various media and that may be impeded by noise*. The aim of this process is to elicit feedback in order to generate a desired effect or outcome.

## Understanding each other

**\*Noise** — anything that interferes, at any stage, with the communication process.

Humans aren't the only beings who communicate – virtually all forms of life are capable of sending and receiving messages. People, however, are the only living organisms known to communicate not just with signals and signs, but through the use of symbols with agreed-upon meanings. If we think about communication as the transfer of meaning, then for each of us, successful communication means that you will understand something just as I do: we are in agreement about what the sender intended and what the receiver ultimately understood.

# Understanding the principles

Communication involves a number of basic principles, which apply across time and cultures. The communication process is always:
• **Dynamic** It is constantly undergoing change.
• **Continuous** Even when you hang up the telephone, you're communicating the message that you have nothing more to say.
• **Circular** Communication is rarely entirely one-way. We each take in information from the outside world, determine what it means, and respond.
• **Unrepeatable** Even if we say something again in precisely the same way, our listeners have heard it before, and so respond to it differently.
• **Irreversible** We cannot "unsay" words.
• **Complex** We all assign slightly different meanings to words. This variation is a product of our backgrounds, education, and experience, and means that there is always the potential for misunderstanding.

**TIP**

**REDUCE NOISE**
The ultimate success of the communication process depends to a large degree on overcoming noise, so make an effort to keep your messages clear, concise, and to the point.

## DEFINING LEVELS OF COMMUNICATION

| LEVEL | AUDIENCE |
| --- | --- |
| Intrapersonal | Communication within ourselves, sending messages to various parts of our bodies, thinking things over, or working silently on a problem. |
| Interpersonal | Communication between or among people, sending messages from one person to another – verbally and nonverbally – with the hope of transferring meaning from one person to another. |
| Organizational | Communication in the context of an organization, sending and receiving messages through various layers of authority and using various channels to discuss topics of interest to the group we belong to or the company we work for. |
| Mass or public | Sending messages from one person or source to many people simultaneously, through television, the internet, or print media. |

# Overcoming barriers

Why do attempts at communication often fail? Broadly speaking, there are two barriers that keep us from communicating successfully: the operations of our bodies and our minds, and our assumptions that other people understand and react to the world in the same way that we do.

## Unblocking your communications

The information we receive about the world comes from our senses. It is possible, however, for our senses to be impaired or for the source of the message to provide inadequate information to be reliably decoded. In sending messages to others, we must be sensitive to the fact that they may not see, hear, touch, taste, or smell in the same way we do.

## Ensuring understanding

Communication is more than sending and receiving messages; if the message has been delivered but not understood, no communication has taken place. Everything, from the culture in which we live to the norms or standards of the groups to which we belong, can influence how we perceive the messages, events, and experiences of everyday life. Even individual mindsets, such as holding stereotypes, can set up barriers, affecting what we understand and how we react to outside stimuli.

**CONSIDER CULTURE**
Be aware that different backgrounds, education, and experience give people different expectations. Your way of seeing the world is not the only one.

   Learn to recognize the barriers likely to block your communications, and focus on what you can do to overcome them. When speaking to someone, for example, constantly monitor their reactions to confirm that you are being fully understood.

## Overcoming barriers to communication

**BANISH PREJUDICE**
Never make a judgement before knowing the facts about a situation. Acknowledge that you are usually working with incomplete data.

**FIGHT STEREOTYPES**
Don't assume that all members of a group share the same characteristics. Put aside any stereotypical views you may have; treat each person as an individual.

**CONTROL YOUR FEELINGS**
Try to present your arguments rationally rather than emotionally, and accept that other people may have strong feelings about a subject.

**WATCH YOUR LANGUAGE**
Recognize that language has different levels of meaning. People will respond differently to the same words, especially if the words are vague or general.

# Communicating at work

Communication is a fundamental skill, central to the human experience. We each know how to do it; we've done it since birth and receive additional practice each day. So why is it so difficult to communicate on the job? As a manager, it is important to understand how the workplace changes the nature of communication for both sender and receiver.

**TIP**

**LOOK ABOVE AND BELOW**

Notice how communication differs throughout your organization and always tailor your message style and content. Is one style of format, content, or message preferred by management, and another by those at more junior levels?

## Tailoring your approach

Several factors in business life alter the way in which we look at communication. We all have a personal communication style, but within an organization you often have to adapt your approach to accommodate the needs of those you work with and work for. If you put the preferences of your audience – particularly your boss and your clients – above your own, you will often get what you want faster. The way you communicate also depends on your position within the organization. The higher your level of responsibility, the more you have to take into account when communicating. And as you become more accountable, you need to keep better records – a form of communication to yourself that may later be read by others.

## ✓ CHECKLIST **ADAPTING YOUR STYLE**

| | YES | NO |
|---|---|---|
| • Do you understand how the culture of the organization you work for affects the way in which you need to communicate? | ☐ | ☐ |
| • Have you adapted your writing and speaking style to the expectations of the culture in which you are working? | ☐ | ☐ |
| • Have you changed your style to accommodate any changes in the structure of the company or the conditions of your industry? | ☐ | ☐ |
| • Have you noted the communication preferences of your supervisor and adapted your writing, speaking, and listening styles accordingly? | ☐ | ☐ |

## Adapting to your environment

Organizations, like the people who work in them, are
in constant flux. Businesses change by necessity with
the conditions of the marketplace and the lives of the
managers who run them. Your communications must
adapt to the conditions in which you find yourself.
However, this never constitutes a reason for signing
your name to a document that is false, or passing
along information that you know isn't true.

## Matching the culture

All communication must work within an organization's
culture. The accepted approach can vary considerably
between different organizations: some companies, for
example, require every issue to be written in memo
form and circulated before it can be raised in a team
meeting. Other organizations are much more "oral"
in nature, offering employees the opportunity to
talk things through before writing anything down.

Many companies rely on a particular culture
to move day-to-day information through the
organization. To succeed in such a business,
you must adapt to the existing culture rather
than try to change it or ask it to adapt to you.

# Planning your approach

Getting people to listen to what you say, read what you write, or look at what you show them isn't easy. How do you persuade them that paying attention to your message is in their best interest? The key to ensuring that your communication hits the mark is detailed planning.

**QUESTION YOUR OWN ROLE**

Ask yourself whether you are the right person to send the message. Will your signature compel people to action, or might the message be more effective coming from your manager, or someone closer to the intended audience?

## Choosing your approach

The choices you make, from the content of the message you send to the medium you select, all have a direct impact on the outcome of your communication. Whatever the situation, ask yourself about the following:

• **Message** What should your message contain? How should your message impart the information? Should your message be broad or detailed?

• **Medium** What's the best way to send this message? Is one medium quicker or cheaper than another? Will one offer a better opportunity for feedback or carry more detail?

• **Code** Will your audience understand the words you've used? Will the words and images mean the same thing to the audience as they mean to you? Do these words and images have multiple meanings for various audiences?

• **Feedback** How will you know if you've communicated successfully? Will the audience response be delayed? Will it be filtered through another source?

• **Noise** How many other senders and messages are out there? Whose message traffic are you competing with? Will others try to deflect, distort, or disable your communication attempts?

• **Effect** What are the goals or communication outcomes you're hoping for? How will you know whether you've achieved them? How will the audience know that the information and ideas you've communicated are useful and worth acting on?

# Targeting your communication

Planning targeted communication involves ensuring that you:

## WORK WITHIN OBJECTIVES
All of your communication should be consistent with and directly supportive of the strategic objectives of your organization – its vision, values, and beliefs.

## ADAPT TO YOUR AUDIENCE
Appeal to the basic needs (shelter, sustenance, safety, companionship, or social approval) of your intended audience or their senses (use motion, colour, and sound). What can you do to hold their attention?

## EXPLAIN YOUR POSITION
Use words that your audience will understand and concepts they can relate to. This means, of course, that you must know who your audience are, as well as what they know and how they feel about the subject.

## MOTIVATE YOUR AUDIENCE
Encourage your audience to accept and act on your message by appealing to authorities that they respect, the social conformity displayed by others they know or admire, the rationality of your argument, or their desire to behave in consistent ways.

## KEEP THEM ON SIDE
Make your audience resistant to counter-persuasion by asking for a tangible, preferably public, commitment from them, or reminding them of the benefits to be derived from doing as you ask.

## MANAGE EXPECTATIONS
Always let your audience know what to expect, and deliver what you promise, never less. People are disappointed only if their expectations exceed what they actually receive.

# Understanding your audience

Who are these people you're communicating with? What do you know about them? What do they know about you or your subject? How do they feel about it? When preparing to communicate, ask a few simple questions about the people in your audience. Once you know more about them, you can find ways to motivate them to listen.

**TIP**

**GET TO KNOW YOUR AUDIENCE**

It's all too easy to stereotype an audience, especially when you are working against the clock. Make sure you have collected all the information available about your audience, and refer to the key characteristics as you prepare your speech or document.

## Pinpointing backgrounds

When you're assessing your audience, look for any similarities in personal backgrounds. For example, what is the average age of audience members? Consider whether they will be familiar with the concepts you plan to speak about, and the sort of life experiences they may have had. Next, think about the education level of your audience. This will have a significant influence on the content of your talk or document, including its central themes and the vocabulary you employ. The personal beliefs of your audience are an important factor to take into account when planning what you will say. Are they liberal or conservative? What is their political affiliation? Are they committed to a particular religious or social point of view?

## Considering ethnicity

The ethnic origin of members of your audience may be worth knowing, but don't overestimate its value. The utility of this information may lie in knowing which issues and positions are of greatest concern to members of a particular ethnic group. The limitation lies in knowing that you cannot reasonably stereotype the views of all members of such a group. Sensitivity to ethnic issues and language styles should be sufficient as you prepare a speech.

# Positioning status

For certain forms of communication, knowing the economic status and lifestyle of your audience is especially important. Gain as much information as you can about the following:

• **Occupation** Knowing how people earn their living will tell you something about their educational background and their daily routines, as well as their motivations and interests.

• **Income** Knowing how much money an audience makes can give you some idea of what their concerns are. The less they make, the more they will be driven by basic needs, such as food and housing. American psychologist Abraham Maslow documented the Hierarchy of Human Needs, showing that higher level needs – such as self-actualization – are only relevant to people once their more basic needs have been met.

• **Socioeconomic status** This term describes where your audience is located in the social/economic spectrum. It is, of course, a direct function of other factors, such as income, education, occupation, neighbourhood, friends, family, and more. Think of this as a single descriptor that explains just how much prestige your audience has in the eyes of others in their own society, and use it to target your words to address their problems, hopes, and needs.

 **IN FOCUS... GENDER TRAITS**

Gender refers to the social and psychological expectations, roles, and views of men and women.

Considerable evidence now indicates that this may be among the least useful pieces of information to know about your audience. Why? Because study after study has shown no statistically significant difference in the responses of professional men and women to a wide range of stimuli. Clearly, knowing that your audience might be composed exclusively of one sex or another might alter your approach somewhat, but you would be unwise to assume that you should communicate in one way for men and another for women.

# Matching the message

Once you know something about the individuals who make up your audience, begin to think about how to approach them. You'll need a strategy to help devise the right message and to choose the most effective method of communication for your audience.

## Hitting the right knowledge level

A thorough knowledge of what your audience already knows about your speaking subject is useful in a number of ways. First, it tells you where to begin. Don't speak down to the audience by explaining fundamentals they already understand. Second, don't start above their heads. Begin at a point they are comfortable with and move on from there.

## GETTING YOUR MESSAGE ACROSS

**FAST TRACK**

**OFF TRACK**

| FAST TRACK | OFF TRACK |
|---|---|
| Knowing as much as you can about who will read or hear your words | Assuming the audience knows all or nothing about your subject |
| Tailoring your message to the needs and interests of your audience | Acting as if the audience already shares your ideas and interests |
| Understanding who the key decision-makers are, and their criteria for making decisions | Failing to check who exactly is in your audience, and what they need to know in order to act |
| Knowing who is respected by your audience and seeking their approval for what you recommend | Assuming your ideas are good enough to stand up on their own, and discussing them with no-one |

# Managing emotions

Even more important than what the audience knows about your subject is how they feel about it. What they know about taxation is far less relevant than how they feel about it when they listen to a talk about tax reform. You need to tailor your words carefully to what the emotional response of your audience is likely to be. The greater the degree of ego involvement (or emotional response) to a given topic, the narrower the range of acceptable positions open to you. In other words, people are much more open-minded on topics they are indifferent about than they are on topics they care about passionately. If you misjudge an emotional response, your communication will fail.

# Establishing the audience's role

Your message may need to reach only the audience before you, or you may be relying on those people to pass on the message to others. Think about everyone who might see or hear your message, including:
• **Primary audience** These are the people who will receive your written or spoken message directly. Make sure that you understand and address their needs, interests, and concerns.
• **Secondary audience** Others might read or hear of your message indirectly. Could the communication be given to a reporter, union organizer, or competitor?
• **Gatekeepers** These are the individuals who you have to route your message through, and who might filter or block it. Does someone in particular stand between you and the audience you hope to reach?
• **Opinion leaders** These are individuals who have significant influence over members of the audience. Who do they admire or listen to on this subject?
• **Key decision-makers** These are people with the power to influence the outcome of the communication.

**HOW TO...
MOTIVATE
YOUR
AUDIENCE**

> Begin by expressing shared values before moving on to more contentious areas.

> Grant a favour to win a concession from an audience.

> Finally, use the promise of reward or the possibility of punishment, if appropriate.

# Choosing your medium

Most managers make decisions about whether to write or speak to someone based on two criteria: convenience and their own personal preferences. But an effective choice of communication medium or channel depends on much more than what suits you at the time.

**TIP**

**TURN OFF THE AUTOMATIC PILOT**
Most of us reach immediately for our preferred form of communication. Learn to stop, consider your options, and purposefully choose the right channel and medium for the message.

## Learning to ignore instinct

Many managers choose a form of communication instinctively, and not always for the right reasons. For example, if you need to pass bad news to a colleague but don't want to provoke a confrontation, you might choose to send an email, even though your colleague would prefer to hear from you in person. On another occasion, you might choose to make a phone call rather than write a letter, because it seems quicker or easier. You might make this choice even when the message is complex and would benefit from extensive explanation, detailed description, or visual aids.

In fact, just two factors should govern your choice of medium for any message. You should think first about the preferences of the person or audience receiving your message, and second about the characteristics and benefits of speaking versus those of writing.

## IN FOCUS... THE PLATINUM RULE

We're all familiar with the old rule: "Do unto others as you would have them do unto you." It's a good rule, but it contains a small flaw. What if others don't want to receive the same treatment as you? What if their preferences are, in fact, significantly different? The Platinum Rule, devised by communication expert Tony

Alessandra, is a variation of that age-old maxim: "Do unto others as they want to be done unto." This means treat others as they want to be treated, not how you think they should be treated. Communicate with others in the manner that they prefer and you'll get what you want: their time, attention, and cooperation.

# Knowing when to write

Writing produces a permanent record, can be used to convey great detail, is often much more precise, and can be used for careful wording. If it's important that you say something in a specific or exact way, you may want to write it down. And, of course, if your audience has a preference for source material or large amounts of detail, such as tables or large lists, you can provide that information as an appendix or attachment to a memo, report, or proposal.

Keep in mind that you may have to share your message with many people and it may be impractical or impossible to speak to each of them. Writing in a precise, persuasive way may be the best approach to influence your audience.

# Identifying when to speak

Speaking provides a richer context – it includes the use of nonverbal cues and allows for more emotion. This communication form is less rigid, as it leaves no permanent record. It may also be much quicker.

Speaking to others also invites their participation. It may be the best way to elicit ideas, size up other people's feelings, and even discover any possible objections to your message before decisions have been made and formalized in writing. Once something is written down, people tend to feel committed to that course of action, even if the documents can easily be revised. A conversation or discussion, on the other hand, has a more transitory feel to it: it is flowing and flexible, and less permanent and formal than written forms of communication.

# Chapter 2

# **Speaking and writing**

Two of the most important skills for a manager, and often also the most daunting, are to stand up in front of an audience and deliver a presentation, and to communicate effectively in writing, whether in formal business letters, email correspondence, or detailed reports. For both, clear thinking, preparation, and practice are the keys to success.

# Planning your speech

Preparing for a business presentation is the most important stage of the process. While it may seem daunting at first, planning your speech becomes much easier once you break the task down into manageable steps, ensuring that you address all the relevant issues at the right time.

## **Defining substance and style**

When it comes to giving a speech, content is king. Substance matters and there is absolutely no substitute for knowing what you're talking about. This means that, whenever possible, you should select a topic that you know and understand, so that you can talk about it with confidence. However, this also depends on your audience; never forget that they are the reason you are in the room. Using your knowledge of your audience to tailor the content to meet their expectations is not a guarantee of success, but it is certainly a step in the right direction.

# Determining your purpose

Before you start to plan the details of your speech, make sure that you know why you are speaking. If you can't come up with a reason for speaking, then don't speak. Identifying your role as a speaker and your importance to the listeners is especially important. It may be that this audience wants your views on the subject at hand and is keenly interested in your opinions. Alternatively, your purpose may be purely to inform them about a topic, and the demand for your opinions may not be as high as you imagine.

Find out, too, all you can about the context in which the presentation will take place. You need to know the answers to questions such as: is your audience still in the fact-gathering stage, or are they ready to make a decision? What is their reason for listening to you? How urgent is the subject you'll be speaking about? Have recent events, either locally or globally, affected their view of the topic in any way? Are your listeners involved in a process that will require them to take action after hearing what you have to say?

**TIP**

**MAKE TIME FOR RESEARCH**
You're being paid for your time preparing and delivering the speech, but the 80:20 rule applies – spend around 80 per cent of your time on research and preparation, and only around 20 per cent on practice and delivery.

## CASE STUDY

### Preparing to succeed

Elizabeth Allen, chief communication officer of the international office supplies firm Staples, Inc., was given the task of drafting a press-conference speech for her CEO, Tom Stemberg, to announce Staples's sponsorship of a new sports arena in Los Angeles. Ms Allen knew that this financial arrangement would be covered by the sports press, not the business press. She also knew that sports figures, civic officials, investors, and reporters would be in the room: "Many people thought the name would be a local, California company.... This was a Boston company putting its name on a Los Angeles landmark. There were cultural factors at work here, as well as political and business factors." As she considered how to prepare the speech, she decided three things: she would reduce her thinking to one or two main points; she would include a few examples and anecdotes that the local audience would relate to; and most importantly, she would cite at least one powerful reason why the relationship between her company and the City of Los Angeles would be productive and long-term.

# Preparing your speech

Once you have a clear picture in your mind of why you are giving the presentation, who your audience is, and what they want to hear from you, start to make a detailed plan of your speech. This planning stage is vital, so make sure that you don't leave it to the last minute. You need to be completely familiar with the structure and content of your speech by the time you deliver it. There are eight key steps to preparing a successful presentation.

## 1 COMPOSE A THESIS STATEMENT

Write a one-sentence declaration of what you want the audience to know, understand, believe, or do. Make it brief, simple, comprehensive, and as complete as possible.

## 2 DEVELOP THE MAIN POINTS

Restrict yourself to just two or three main points, so that you will have time to explain and support them all. Make sure that all of your evidence relates to and is supportive of your principal reason for speaking.

## 5 PREPARE YOUR OUTLINE

Write a one-page outline of your speech. Think about the issues you plan to raise, the sequence in which you will address each of them, and the evidence you'll offer your audience in support of those ideas.

## 6 CONSIDER VISUALS

Think about what visuals will best enhance your speech, by helping to explain, reinforce, and clarify your main points. Sometimes it is easier to show the audience something than to say it.

# Steps to preparing a speech

**3 GATHER SUPPORTING MATERIALS**
Now gather evidence to support your main points. Use your knowledge of the audience to select the kinds of proof that they will find most convincing. Make your evidence compelling, recent, and fully transparent to your listeners.

**4 THINK ABOUT STRUCTURE**
Consider the order in which you will deliver the information, and think about what you will say in your introduction, in the body of the speech, and in your conclusion.

**7 WRITE THE SPEECH**
Now prepare the content of your speech in detail. Some people choose to write in short bullet points, others write their script out more fully. Choose the way that best suits you, but remember that your audience want to hear you speak to them, not read to them.

**8 PREPARE YOUR NOTES**
Finally, transfer your speech into the notes you will use to deliver it. These may be bullet points on a PowerPoint presentation, written notes on notecards, or the full manuscript.

# Developing visual support

Behavioural scientists have known for many years that visual images can have a powerful effect on the process of learning. In some cases, pictures may reach people who simply don't listen well to the spoken word, or who may not understand what the words mean.

**TIP**

**CHOOSE THE RIGHT CHART**

Charts and graphs are a useful way to display data. Be sure to select the type of chart (such as a pie chart, bar chart, or line graph) that most clearly illustrates any comparisons you want to make, and use colour carefully to emphasize your point.

## How does visual support help?

Behavioural scientists have found that visual support is important in communication for three main reasons:
• It can help explain, reinforce, and clarify the spoken word during a presentation. If you can't say something easily, you may be able to show it to your audience.
• Some people pay more attention to what they see than what they hear, and can more quickly and easily recall information and concepts with a visual component than those that are just spoken aloud.
• People tend to recognize ideas most easily when they are presented as a combination of both words and pictures, rather than when presented as either words or pictures alone.

## Choosing when to use it

Displaying information in a visual manner will enhance most presentations, but tends to work best:
• When you have new data for your audience
• When the information you hope to convey is complex or technical in nature
• If your message is coming to the audience in a new context
• For certain types of information – such as numbers, quick facts, quotes, and lists
• For explaining relationships or comparisons
• For revealing geographical or spatial patterns.

# Using visuals effectively

Good visuals have a number of characteristics in common. The most important is simplicity. The more complex a visual display becomes, the more difficult it is for an audience to understand. Keep your visuals clear, ordered, and simple when trying to explain an important idea or relationship.

Good visuals use colour to explain and attract. Very few people tend to have exactly the same taste in colours, but almost everyone appreciates occasions when colours are used meaningfully and consistently. Certain traditions, such as using red numbers or bars to indicate a loss and black ones to indicate profit, allow audiences to quickly grasp information. Try using a simple legend to explain colour use on your charts and graphs; it helps the audience and will ensure consistency and simplicity in your visual aids.

## USING VISUALS WELL

**FAST TRACK**

**OFF TRACK**

| FAST TRACK | OFF TRACK |
| --- | --- |
| Thinking carefully about the needs and interests of your audience as you plan your visual aids | Including large amounts of text in your visuals so the audience has to read much of your message |
| Choosing visuals that capture the essence of your main points | Using stock visuals that are only indirectly related to your main points |
| Using colour in a consistent, careful manner so that related items are colour-coded and grouped together | Failing to explain any coding in your visuals, including your use of colour, symbols, and graphic depictions |
| Making sure your visual support is simple, crisp, clean, and uncluttered | Not worrying about the overall look and hoping it will work adequately |

# Improving your confidence

It's one thing to know your material. It's another matter entirely to believe that you can get up on stage and speak with confidence to a group of strangers. Understanding your message and having a well-organized speech are important to your success, but so is self-confidence.

**TIP**

**KEEP NOTES SIMPLE**

Losing your place in lengthy notes can give your confidence a serious knock, so make sure your notes are quick and easy to use, giving you the information you need at a glance.

## Improving your delivery

Rehearsal will help improve your speech and raise your level of self-confidence. Simply knowing that you've been through the contents of your speech more than once builds familiarity and is reassuring. It will also ensure you talk for the correct amount of time. A run-through or two will show whether you have too much, too little, or just enough to say. Rehearsal will also help you to improve your transitions. By practising your speech, you'll be able to identify the rough spots and work on smoothing the transition from one main point to another and from one part of the speech to another.

## Using notes

The best speakers seem to confidently deliver their speeches extemporaneously, or "from the heart", without notes. Such speeches aren't really memorized word-for-word, but rather are thoroughly researched, well rehearsed, and professionally supported. Many extemporaneous speakers will use their visual support – acetate transparencies, 35-mm slides, or electronic slides – to prompt their memories. Others prefer to work from bullet points on notecards, or use the full manuscript. Whichever you choose, make sure that your notes are simple, easy to follow, and allow you to maintain eye contact with the audience.

# Gaining confidence

The better prepared you are, the more confident you will feel at the podium. Make sure you have thought about all aspects of your presentation, from the layout of the room to the type of microphone you will use. The knowledge that you have personally arranged every detail, and have meticulously planned and rehearsed your talk, will help build your confidence. If you get cold feet, remember that you've been asked to speak because the audience is interested in your expertise and viewpoint. Just approach this speech as you would any other managerial task, knowing that you have the ability, the intelligence, and the confidence to get it done.

**"The audience wants to hear what I have to say."**

**"I'm the expert. I know this subject better than anyone."**

**"I know my speech, and I'm confident that it reads and flows easily and well."**

## ✓ CHECKLIST BEING PREPARED

| | YES | NO |
|---|---|---|
| • Have you double-checked the time and location for your speech? | ☐ | ☐ |
| • Are you sure about the length of time allotted to the speech? | ☐ | ☐ |
| • Have you decided how to arrange the room? | ☐ | ☐ |
| • Have you found out whether you are using a lectern or are free to walk around the room during the speech? | ☐ | ☐ |
| • Have you tested the microphone and sound system? | ☐ | ☐ |
| • Are you familiar with the arrangements and systems for visuals? | ☐ | ☐ |
| • Do you know what lighting is available, and have you planned whether it needs to change for screen visuals or handouts during your talk? | ☐ | ☐ |
| • If you are using a computer during the presentation, are the relevant files backed-up on a second computer to use if necessary? | ☐ | ☐ |

# Delivering your speech

You've researched the topic thoroughly, written and organized your thoughts, and rehearsed your remarks. Use the confidence that you've developed in planning and rehearsal to take the next step: get up and speak. You are the medium, or bearer, of the message, and your delivery is critical to the successful communication of your ideas.

## Improving your delivery

As you approach the challenge of becoming an accomplished public speaker, keep in mind that no-one is born with great public-speaking ability. Language is the habit of a lifetime, and your ability to speak with conviction and sincerity is a function of your willingness to work at it. Your skills will improve with every speech that you make, and as you master the art of presentation, chances are that others in a position of influence will and reward you for your effort.

### CASE STUDY

#### Capturing audiences

How does Apple Computer CEO Steve Jobs garner so much attention when he speaks at industry events and product launches? Much of his ability to mesmerize a crowd comes from his methodical preparation and passion for the subject. "Jobs over-prepares and knows his material cold, so his mind is free to do audience calibration," says Bill Cole, CEO of Procoach Systems in San Jose, California, US. "He reads the audience instead of being in his head, remembering what to do or say next. He knows his material and mechanics so well that he can go with the flow." In 2005, Jobs gave the commencement speech at Stanford University. He centred his talk on stories about his life, such as being given up as a newborn for adoption, dropping out of college, founding the Apple Computer company, and then getting fired from his very own company. "His personal stories are brief and powerful," says Ginny Pulos, a communication consultant from New York. "You can see the emotion on his face and hear it in his words." The lesson for executives, says Pulos, is to "learn to tell stories about the passions in your life."

## Ways to keep your audience interested

### MAKE A CONNECTION
- Step up to the lectern, breathe deeply, smile, think positively, and speak
- Humanize and personalize your speech – share your experiences, values, goals, and fears
- Do your best to be one of them (unless it's clear you are not)
- Use humour where appropriate (unless you are not funny)
- Actively involve the audience as much as you can
- Focus on current local events and issues known to the audience

### HELP THEM UNDERSTAND
- Blueprint the speech: tell the audience where your talk is going
- Begin with the familiar, then move to the unfamiliar
- Talk process first, then add in the detail
- Visualize and demonstrate your ideas where you can
- Use interim summaries and transitions to guide your audience through what you have to say
- Give examples to illustrate your concepts and ideas
- Tell stories, and dramatize your central theme

# Becoming a better writer

Very few people think writing is easy. Good writing – that is, writing with power, grace, dignity, and impact – takes time, careful thought, and revision. Such writing is often the product of many years of training and practice. Even though writing may sometimes seem like hard work, with a little effort you can learn to do it well.

**ALWAYS EDIT**
Revising and editing are critical to good writing. Putting some time between writing and editing will help you be more objective. Revise your writing with the intent to simplify, clarify, and trim excess words.

## Organizing your writing

Good business writing is simple, clear, and concise. By not calling attention to itself, good writing is "transparent", helping the reader focus on the idea you are trying to communicate rather than on the words that you are using to describe it.

The key to good business writing is organization. You need to know where you are going before you start, so do your research and identify the key issues you need to cover. Compose a list of the most important points, and use them to create an outline. If your document will include an overview section containing your purpose for writing, write this first. Next, tackle the most important paragraphs, before filling out the details and any supplementary material.

## ? ASK YOURSELF... HAVE I EXPLAINED ADEQUATELY?

- Does my writing flow in a logical way, and have I given complex explanations in a step-by-step form?
- Have I "translated" any technical terms?
- Have I said enough to answer questions and allay fears without giving too much detail?
- Have I used visuals to help explain complex facts?
- Have I cautioned the reader, where necessary, against common mistakes and misreading of the information?

# Meeting your reader's needs

Before you write, find out what the reader expects, wants, and needs. If you later discover that you must deviate from these guidelines, let the reader know why. When composing your document, don't include material that you don't need: you may be accused of missing the point. Make sure, too, that you always separate facts from opinions in your writing. The reader should never be in doubt as to what you know to be true, and what you think may be the case. Always apply a consistent approach to avoid misunderstandings.

# Writing for clarity

When composing a memo, letter, or report, keep in mind that your reader often doesn't have much time: senior managers, in particular, generally have tight schedules and too much to read. They need your written communication to quickly and clearly give them the details they need to know.

Ensure that your writing style is both precise and concise. Use simple, down-to-earth words, and avoid needless ones and wordy expressions. Simple words and expressions are more quickly understood and can add power to your ideas. Be direct, and avoid vague terms such as "very" and "slightly"; this will show that you have confidence in what you are saying and will add power to your ideas. Make sure, too, that everything you write is grammatically correct – you don't want your busy reader to have to re-read your sentences to try to decipher their meaning.

Keep your paragraphs short; they are more inviting and more likely to get read. If your document must include numbers, use them with restraint – a paragraph filled with numbers can be difficult to read and follow. Use a few numbers selectively to make your point, then put the rest in tables and graphics.

**TIP**

**MAKE IT PERFECT**
Eliminate factual errors, typos, misspellings, bad grammar, and incorrect punctuation in your writing. Remember that if one detail in a memo you have written is recognized to be incorrect, your entire line of thinking may be considered suspect.

# Making your writing come alive

To escape from outdated, excessively formal writing styles, try to make your writing more like your speaking, and then "tidy it up". Imagine your reader is in front of you and aim all the time for writing that is clear, fresh, and easy to read. You may need to write a first draft for structural purposes, and then go back over your document. Make sure that your writing is:

• **Vigorous and direct** Use active sentences and avoid the passive voice. Be more definite by limiting the use of the word "not".

• **Free of clichés and jargon** Tired, hackneyed words and expressions make your writing appear superficial.

• **Made up of short sentences** This won't guarantee clarity, but short sentences will prevent many of the confusions that can easily occur in longer ones. Try the ear test: read your writing aloud and break apart any sentence you can't finish in one breath.

• **Connecting with the reader** Reach out to your reader by occasionally using questions. A request gains emphasis when it ends with a question mark. Rather than writing, "Please advise as to whether the meeting is still scheduled for February 21st", simply ask: "Is the meeting still scheduled for February 21st?"

> **WRITE WITH PERSONAL PRONOUNS**
> Use "we", "us", and "our" when speaking for the company. Use "I", "me", and "my" when speaking for yourself. Either way, be generous with the use of the word "you".

## IN FOCUS... THE RIGHT ORDER

A poorly organized letter reads like a mystery story. Clue by clue, it unfolds details that make sense only towards the end – if the reader makes it that far. Your job is to make it easier for the reader, by explaining each point with an overview, followed by details. To avoid any confusion, always give directions before reasons, requests before justifications, answers before explanations, conclusions before details, and solutions before problems. Try the approach used in newspaper articles. They start with the most important information and taper off to the least important.

**USE CONTRACTIONS**
Make your writing softer and more accessible by occasionally using the contractions that we naturally speak with, such as "I'm", "we're", "you'd", "they've", "can't", "don't", and "let's".

**ALLOW SENTENCES TO END WITH A PREPOSITION**
Don't reword a sentence just to move a preposition (e.g. "after", "at", "by", "from", "of", "to", or "up") from the end. You are likely to lengthen, tangle, and stiffen the sentence.

**Capturing and keeping your readers' attention**

**USE SHORT TRANSITIONS**
Use "but" more than "however", and "more than" rather than "in addition to". Use more formal transitions only for variety. Don't be afraid to start a sentence with words like "but", "so", "yet", "and", or "or".

**USE THE PRESENT TENSE WHENEVER POSSIBLE**
This adds immediacy to your writing. Be careful, however, not to slip from the present to the past tense and back again, as this will make your writing confusing. Select one tense and stick to it.

# Writing a business letter

Business letters are primarily external documents, although managers will occasionally use letters to correspond with subordinates and executives within their organization. Good letters are crisp, concise, and organized so that readers can follow and understand the content with little effort.

**TIP**

**BE PROMPT**
When you receive a business letter, always send an answer within three business days. If you can't reply within this time – because you need to speak with someone else or gather information – drop the writer a note to let them know that you are working on their problem.

## Writing successful letters

Your success as a business writer depends, in large measure, on your ability to convince others that what you have written is worth their attention. This is more likely if your letter meets three criteria: it should be compact, it should be informal, and it absolutely must be organized. Be careful, however. Brevity is desirable, but you can overdo it. Make sure that your letters are not too brief or curt. It is extremely important to make sure that your reader has enough information to understand the subject. Include each issue relevant to the subject, and explain the process, the outcome, or the decision to the satisfaction of the reader. If you were receiving the letter, would the information be sufficient? Would you be satisfied that the writer had taken you seriously?

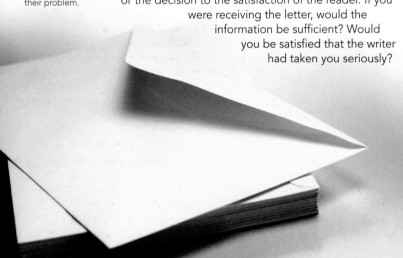

# Showing interest

When writing in response to a letter you have received, aim to show that you are genuinely interested. The person writing to you thought the issue was important enough to write about; you should think so, too. Show by your words and actions that you care about them and the issue they've written about.

Give everyone the benefit of the doubt. Don't automatically assume that the person corresponding with you is doing so for the purpose of cheating you or your company.

## IN FOCUS...
### FORM LETTERS

It may be tempting to compile a "one-size-fits-all" approach to writing when there are many recipients, but it is usually a recipe for disaster. A letter must answer all of the questions its audience is likely to have, responding to their fears, doubts, and concerns. In situations in which it is absolutely necessary to use this approach, you can test market form letters, by showing them to several people who are (or have been) members of the audience in question and asking for suggestions for improvement.

# Hitting the right tone

If a correspondent makes (or attempts) a joke, play along. Show that you have a sense of humour. Racist, sexist, or profane humour is never appropriate, but ordinary self-deprecating or directionless humour can often lighten or improve a difficult situation.

If you have to deliver bad news by letter, say you are sorry. Use phrases such as, "I am sorry to say that…" or "I regret to say that we'll be unable to [do something] because…". You can soften the blow by saying that you're sorry it happened, or that you regret the outcome. If it's bad news and your reader thinks you don't care, you

may spark an unwanted reaction. If you're bearing good news, say that you are glad: "I am delighted to tell you that…". Alternatively use a phrase such as: "You will be pleased to learn that…".

Never write and quickly send off an angry letter. Venting your spleen in an angry, hostile reply to someone may make you feel good, but it's almost never a good idea to post such a letter. Take your time and cool down before you compose an angry letter. Then, if you have written something you aren't sure about, wait until the following day so that you can re-read what you have written before sending it. Chances are, you'll think twice about posting.

# Using email effectively

Email is now a global means of staying in touch, passing data and graphics, and managing the flow of information needed to run a business. It's also a gateway for unwanted spam and viruses. Properly managed, though, email can become a productivity booster, a link to distant markets, and an essential communication tool.

**TIP**

**ESTABLISH A RESPONSE TIME**

If you usually respond to email messages immediately, people grow to expect an immediate response, and become annoyed if you differ from this. The rule of thumb in business is to respond to emails by the end of the same day. If it's really urgent, use the telephone instead.

## Reducing your emailing time

Email is a tool; don't let it become your master. Limit the time you spend on email by following these tips:

• **Send less, get less** Think carefully about whether you really need to draft new messages or respond to those you've already received.

• **Escape the endless reply loop** Silence in response to an email message may feel rude, but is acceptable. If you wish to reassure someone that no reply is necessary, finish a message with "no reply needed," or a request with "Thanks in advance." Avoid asking any questions for which you don't really want or need answers.

• **Think twice about the "cc" box** If you copy in a large number of people to your emails and they all respond with a reply that needs an answer, your message backlog may become unmanageable.

## ✓ CHECKLIST **KNOWING WHEN EMAIL IS INAPPROPRIATE**

| | YES | NO |
|---|---|---|
| • Do I need to convey or discern emotion? | ☐ | ☐ |
| • Do I need to cut through the communication clutter? | ☐ | ☐ |
| • Do I need to move quickly? | ☐ | ☐ |
| • Do I want a remote communication to be private? | ☐ | ☐ |
| • Am I trying to reach someone who doesn't have (or check) email? | ☐ | ☐ |
| • Do I want to engage people and get an immediate response? | ☐ | ☐ |

# Improving your habits

Don't check your email constantly. Check it at regular intervals, such as first thing in the morning, once after lunch, and again before going home. Be disciplined about your email management. Aim to handle each message just once. If it's unimportant or irrelevant, hit the delete key. If you spend more than three hours a week sorting through junk mail, you have a problem and need to reorganize your system.

If a message is something you'll need to respond to, decide whether to do it now or later, when you will have the time and information you need. Once you have responded, move the message out of your inbox and into an archive folder.

# Avoiding the pitfalls

It's all too easy to send an email quickly, only to regret it later. Before sending any email, always check the "To" field before you click "Send". Make sure you're sending this message to the address you intend. Double-check to make absolutely certain you haven't clicked "Reply All".

Make sure your computer – and your company's email server – are set to the correct time and date. Messages with an incorrect time or date can be misfiled or overlooked.

## HOW TO...
## SEND A BETTER EMAIL

Pick the subject line of the email carefully: make it informative and brief so the recipient can easily find and act on it.

Now write the main body of the email, using correct grammar, punctuation, and capitalization.

Avoid abbreviations and cyberjargon: most business professionals dislike them. WIDLTO (when in doubt, leave them out).

Be careful with criticism: be sure to provide enough context and background to avoid a misunderstanding.

Keep it short. If you need more than three paragraphs, phone instead or send the material as an attachment.

Use a signature to conclude your email, but keep it simple: don't be tempted to add humourous or "inspiring" quotes.

Before you send the email, check your attachments. Send only those that your recipient needs or wants to see.

# Writing reports

Reports are longer and more comprehensive than most documents, and are written for the purpose of documenting actions, describing projects and events, and capturing information on complex issues. They are often written by more than one person for audiences with multiple needs and interests.

**INCLUDE A COVER LETTER**

As a courtesy to your reader, always include a cover letter to accompany the report, explaining what the report covers and why. Where appropriate, include the report's most important recommendations or findings.

## Planning your report

There are four main questions to consider when compiling a report:

- **Who is in your audience?** Think about their level of interest in the content, and their familiarity with the issues, ideas, and vocabulary you plan to use.
- **What is the ideal format?** Consider how your readers will use the document – will they start from the beginning and read through page by page, or will they skip to sections that interest them most?
- **Have you collected the right information?** Make sure your information is relevant, correct, and sufficient, and that you know how to explain it most usefully.
- **Is the document properly organized?** Consider using a bold typeface for headings and sub-headings to help organize the information and make it retrievable.

## Writing the report

Reports are divided into three sections: front matter (including title page, abstract, table of contents, and list of figures and tables), the main body of the report, and end matter (bibliography, appendices, glossary, and index). Begin the main body with an executive summary, detailing the report's key points and recommendations. Busy executives may only read this section, so it must tell them all they need to know in order for them to agree with your recommendations.

## DIVIDING YOUR REPORT INTO SECTIONS

| SECTION | CONTENT |
|---|---|
| **Title page** | A single page, containing the full title of the report, the names of the authors, the date on which the report was issued, the name of the organization, and often the people or organization to whom the report is submitted. |
| **Abstract** | A paragraph that briefly summarizes and highlights the major points. Its primary function is to enable a reader to decide whether to read the entire work. |
| **Table of contents** | A list of all of the headings within the report in the order of their appearance, along with a page number for each. |
| **List of figures and tables** | When a report contains more than five figures or tables, it should include a page listing each by title, with page numbers. |
| **Foreword (optional)** | An introductory statement usually written by an authority figure who will be well recognized by prospective readers. It provides background information and places the report in the context of other works in the field. |
| **Preface (optional)** | This describes the purpose, background, or scope of the report. It is sometimes used to acknowledge assistance provided in research or preparation, and sources used. |
| **Executive summary** | This provides more information than the abstract, and enables readers to quickly scan the report's primary points. Executive summaries are usually restricted to a few pages. |
| **Main text** | This forms the main body of the report, and explains your work and its findings. |
| **Conclusion** | This contains not only concluding remarks but also any recommended actions for the readers. |
| **Bibliography** | An alphabetical listing of all the sources you consulted to prepare the report; this suggests additional resources the reader may wish to consult. |
| **Appendices** | Information that supplements the main report as evidence, such as lists, tables of figures, and charts and graphs. |
| **Glossary** | An alphabetical list of definitions of unusual terms used. |
| **Index** | An alphabetical list of topics with page numbers. |

# Chapter 3

# Communicating with your team

A team is only as good as its communication; misunderstandings can cause a huge amount of extra work and lost time. When managing a team, focus on giving constructive feedback, briefing thoroughly, and dealing effectively with conflict.

## Listening effectively

Studies show that adults now spend more than half of their daily communication time listening to someone else speak. As a manager, being able to listen effectively and understand others is at the heart of creating a team that performs to the best of its ability.

### Learning when to listen

Listening is a skill you acquire naturally, but can improve upon if you're motivated to do so. The first step towards becoming a better listener is, surprisingly, to stop. You need to stop talking, stop trying to carry on more than one conversation, and stop interrupting. Let the other person speak. As others are talking, allow yourself to respond cognitively and emotionally, taking in the factual information and the tone of their remarks, without responding. Then ask carefully thought-out questions that will clarify what they have said and reassure you of its basis in fact.

# Getting the message

Start by trying to see things from the speaker's point of view, and let your actions demonstrate this. Show interest with your body language: look the speaker in the eyes and maintain an open and non-threatening posture. Give the speaker physical signs of your undivided attention: close the door, hold your calls, and put aside whatever you're working on.

Listen carefully to how something is said: look out for hints of sarcasm, cynicism, or irony in what you hear. Try to tune in to the speaker's mood and intention. Remember that communication is a shared responsibility, so it is up to you to ensure that you understand the message.

Once you have listened to what a person has to say and clarified anything you're not sure of, evaluate the facts and evidence. Ask yourself whether the evidence is recent, reliable, accurate, and relevant.

**BEWARE WISHFUL THINKING**

Just because you want to hear something doesn't mean it is what the speaker is actually saying. It is all too easy to fall into the trap of selective hearing, so make sure that you listen to everything that the speaker is telling you.

## LISTENING ACTIVELY

| FAST TRACK | OFF TRACK |
|---|---|
| Listening regularly to difficult material to hone your listening ability | Assuming that everything interesting should be provided in written form |
| Giving your full and undivided attention to the speaker | Pretending to listen while actually doing something else |
| Listening to the argument in the speaker's terms, and in the order he or she wishes to follow | Criticizing the speaker's delivery and interrupting the flow of what they are saying to ask questions |
| Focusing on the reasons for the speaker's approach and discussion | Assuming you already know what the issue is and how to resolve it |

# Giving feedback

When he was mayor of New York City, Ed Koch frequently walked the streets of his hometown asking his constituents, "How am I doing?" The question wasn't simply rhetorical. He asked the question of friend and foe alike, and he cared about the responses, because his performance as mayor depended on feedback – direct, honest, current, unfiltered feedback.

## Knowing when to give feedback

Good feedback doesn't just happen. It is the product of careful, deliberate communication strategies, coupled with good interpersonal communication skills. You can significantly increase the probability that the feedback you give helps others to improve by understanding the role of feedback in both personal and professional settings.

Feedback is vital to any organization committed to improving itself, because it is the only way for managers and executives to know what needs to be improved. Giving and receiving feedback should be more than just a part of an employee's behaviour; it should be a part of the whole organization's culture.

## IN FOCUS... LANGUAGE

Not everyone has the same understanding of language, and certain words, phrases, or terms that mean one thing to a manager may mean something very different to a person receiving feedback. It is important, therefore, that the language used for feedback is acceptable to the person being spoken to and appropriate for the circumstances. The words used must be clearly understood and agreed upon by both parties. Acronyms or company jargon are only acceptable if it is clear that both parties know what they mean. Successful managers make sure they know whether the person they are giving feedback to shares the same frame of reference they do, avoid language that will cause confusion, and choose words that are universally understood.

# Knowing how to give feedback

Providing constructive, useful feedback involves more than simply responding to people as they speak to you. Consider the context in which the communication takes place, people's intentions as they speak (or choose not to speak), and your objectives as a manager.

• **Get the timing right** Before deciding to offer feedback, decide whether the moment is right for both people involved. Constructive feedback can happen only within a context of listening to and caring about the other person. If the time isn't right, if the moment isn't appropriate, you can always delay briefly before offering your thoughts.

• **Understand the context** This is the most important characteristic of feedback: find out where an event happened, why it happened, and what led up to it. Always review the actions and decisions that led up to the moment; never simply give feedback and leave.

• **Give both positive and negative feedback** People are more likely to pay attention to your complaints if they have also received your compliments. It is important to remember to tell people when they have done something well.

**TIP**

**FOCUS ON BEHAVIOUR**

If you are giving negative feedback, defuse any hostility and minimize the fear felt by the other person by depersonalizing the conversation: focusing your comments on the behaviour involved, not the people.

## Hitting the right tone

"Why can't you fill out trip reports properly?"

"These trip reports need more detail."

"You've messed up again. Fix it."

"There are errors in this report. Can we talk about it?"

# Understanding nonverbal communication

Most of the meaning transferred from one person to another in a personal conversation comes not from the words that are spoken, but from nonverbal signals. Learning to read, understand, and use these wordless messages isn't easy, but is essential for effective communication.

## Reading nonverbal signals

The movement, positioning, and use of the human body in various communication settings serves a number of functions:
• To highlight or emphasize some part of a verbal message
• To regulate the flow, pace, and back-and-forth nature of verbal messages
• To reinforce the general tone or attitude of a message
• To repeat what the verbal messages convey (holding up three fingers to indicate the number three, for example)
• To substitute for, or take the place of, verbal messages (such as giving a "thumbs up" gesture).

**USE VOCAL DYNAMICS**
Tone, volume, rate, pitch, forcefulness, and enunciation all convey meaning about a subject, and how you feel about the people in the room.

Nonverbal cues are often difficult to read, especially because there are few body movements or gestures that have universally agreed-upon meanings. A colleague who looks tired or overworked to one person may appear disinterested or indifferent to another. While looking for meaning in a particular movement, position, or gesture, be careful not to miss more important signals that reveal the true feelings of a speaker. Body language can sometimes contradict the verbal messages being sent. Tears in a person's eyes, for example, might involuntarily contradict a message telling you that they are fine.

# Using nonverbal signals

**WATCH YOUR APPEARANCE**
Make sure that your clothing and grooming are appropriate to your audience, your reasons for communicating, and the occasion.

**RESTRAIN YOUR MOVEMENTS**
Small gestures, close to your body, will convey an image of confidence and authority. Keep your voice low but audible and your posture relaxed.

**WATCH YOUR EYE CONTACT**
Eye contact usually reinforces trust; however, in some Asian cultures, looking a superior in the eye as you speak can be considered disrespectful.

**TAKE CARE WITH TOUCH**
The rules on touching others in a business context vary from culture to culture. Make sure you know and respect local customs.

# Running briefings and meetings

Briefings and meetings are an inescapable part of business life. They are a means of sharing information, initiating strategies, perpetuating a culture, and building consensus around business goals. Done well, they're good for business and good for morale.

**TIP**

**ANTICIPATE QUESTIONS**

Do your best to address audience concerns, questions, doubts, and fears in advance. Plan the content of your briefing around the needs of those in the audience.

## Organizing a meeting

Be clear about the purpose of any meeting before you start planning. Invite only those people who are directly related to your goals, and make sure you include all the key decision-makers. Once you've arranged a time, place, and date that is convenient to everyone, send them all an agenda, making clear the meeting's theme and goals. In putting together the agenda, consider the following questions: What do we need to do in this meeting? What conversations will be important to those who attend? What information will we need to begin?

Prioritize the most important items so they will be discussed early on in the meeting, and assign a certain amount of time for each agenda item.

## ❓ ASK YOURSELF... DO I NEED TO CALL A MEETING?

- Do I need to motivate people, giving them a "jumpstart" to get going?
- Do I need to share general company or market information with people to help them do their jobs?
- Do I need to initiate a new programme or project?
- Do I wish to introduce people to one another, so they can benefit from each other's experiences?

# Giving a briefing

Briefing is a process by which you provide information to those who need it. As with any form of communication, think about your audience, your purpose, and the occasion. Find out all you can about the audience, and what they hope to take away from the session. State your purpose clearly and simply at the beginning of the meeting: "The purpose of this briefing is to look at budget projections for the next 90 days." Let them know why you're calling the meeting now.

# Delivering a brief

When giving a briefing meeting, choose the form of delivery that best suits your speaking style and the needs of the audience. There are three forms to choose from:

• **Memorized presentations** These are delivered verbatim, just as you wrote them. This gives you total control over the material, but unless you're a trained actor, there's a risk that you'll sound wooden and the material contrived. Worse yet, you may forget where you are and have to start again or refer to notes.

• **Scripted briefings** These are more common, but they can also sound stilted. The problem with reading is that you risk losing eye contact, lowering your chin, and

**CASE STUDY**

**A competitive advantage**
As CEO of the international retail giant Wal-Mart, David Glass knew the company would have to be quick off the mark with merchandising strategies, particularly in response to moves made by competitors. Each Saturday morning, when sales results for the week were transmitted to the corporate headquarters, Glass would gather key subordinates to share information from people in the field. They would tell the sales team what their competitors were doing; the senior team would then focus on corrective actions they wanted to take.

By noon, regional managers would telephone district managers, and each would exchange ideas on the direction they wanted to take that week, along with changes they would implement. "By noon on Saturday," Glass said, "we had all our corrections in place. Our competitors, for the most part, got their sales results on Monday for the week prior. They were already 10 days behind."

compressing your vocal pitch. If you do use a script, rehearse carefully and look up frequently, making regular eye contact with your audience.

• **Extemporaneous briefings** These are delivered either without notes or with visual aids to prompt your memory. They are the most effective choice, looking more spontaneous, while actually being thoroughly researched, tightly organized, and well rehearsed.

# Communicating to persuade

Most successful attempts at persuasion involve four separate, yet related, steps. Following these steps won't guarantee success with any particular audience, but they will set the stage for the attitudes you're trying to shape in your team and the behaviour you hope will follow.

**TIP**

**TELL THEM ABOUT THE BENEFITS**

Make sure you cover the WIIFM question: "What's in it for me?". Don't just tell your team what you want them to do – make sure they understand the many ways in which they themselves will benefit from it.

## Getting their attention

If you want to motivate people to do something, you first have to catch their attention. Research shows that we selectively choose what to pay attention to, both as a defence mechanism against sensory overload, and because we seek out messages with particular value for us. We ignore virtually everything else. There are two ways to capture attention:
• Use physical stimuli, such as bright lights, sound, motion, or colour
• Present stimuli that relate directly to the needs or goals of those you want to persuade.

## Providing a motivation

Next, you need to provide a reason for people to act. A persuasive writer or speaker is one who can lead others to believe in what he or she is advocating, and then encourage some form of behaviour in line with that belief. This amounts to giving good reasons for what you believe. These are not reasons you think are good, but reasons your team thinks are good.

Identify the needs and interests of your team and connect them to your message. Which of their needs are you fulfilling? Appeal to their sense of rationality – show why it makes sense to act on your message. Or call on their sense of conformity, by showing how well others will view them if they act on your message.

# Moving others to act

Once you have captured the attention of those you want to persuade and have given them good cause to believe the message, you must provide them with a clear channel for action. First, however, take time to reassure them: show them that there is a high probability that you can deliver on the promised reward. Your team needs to know that what you've promised will actually come true.

Next, recommend a specific proposal for action. Tell your team exactly what you want them to do, describe how you would like them to go about it, and set out a realistic timescale. Make sure that everyone on your team knows how and when progress will be measured and identify the end point and the rewards for achievement that lie ahead.

# Keeping them on side

The arguments that you use to persuade others can be one-sided, presenting your case alone, or two-sided, presenting your case as well as dealing with real and potential counter-arguments. Choose your approach based on the knowledge and preconceptions of your audience. If you decide to use a two-sided argument, you should:
• Warn your team that others may try to influence them to change their minds.
• State some opposing arguments and then refute them. If you are aware of an opposing message, consider previewing at least part of it to the audience and then explaining why it is flawed.
• Encourage commitment in some tangible or visible way. It's more difficult for someone to back away from a position for which they've publicly proclaimed their support.

## WHEN TO USE ONE- OR TWO-SIDED ARGUMENTS

| ONE-SIDED ARGUMENT | TWO-SIDED ARGUMENT |
| --- | --- |
| The audience initially agrees with you and your aim is simply to intensify support. | You suspect or know that the audience initially disagrees with your position. |
| The audience will not be exposed to any form of counter-persuasion. | You know the audience will be exposed to subsequent counter-persuasion. |
| The audience is not well-educated or may become easily confused by an opponent's argument or evidence. | You hope to produce a more enduring result with a knowledgeable audience. |

# Managing conflict

Conflict* can arise from a variety of sources, but many experts see it as a function of such workplace issues as personality, personal and professional relationships, cultural differences, working environments, demands of the marketplace, and of course, competition. As organizations increasingly use teamwork, differences among team members can lead to conflict.

*Conflict* — a state of opposition or hostilities between two or more people that may arise as a result of clashing principles or incompatible wishes.

## Identifying the sources of conflict

Not all conflict within an organization is unhealthy, but conflict between and among people within an organization can quickly become counter-productive, divisive, and destructive if not properly managed.

Conflict may develop over any number of issues or factors, but these five appear regularly:

• **Limited resources** Everything from office space to budgets may put people in competition with one another. Allocate scarce resources fairly to avoid this.

• **Values, goals, and priorities** Confrontation can occur when people in an organization don't agree on strategic direction or basic priorities. Agreement on goals, large and small, can help to avoid this.

• **Poorly defined responsibilities** Conflict may result from differences between formal position descriptions and daily expectations of the job. Review and agree who is responsible for what (and to whom).

• **Change** Many changes, including those to annual budgets, organizational priorities, lines of authority, or limits of responsibility, as well as restructuring, mergers, divestitures, and lay-offs, can create anxiety, uncertainty, and conflict in an organization.

• **Human drive for success** Conflicts can arise as a result of the natural sense of goal orientation that every human experiences. Many organizations actively foster a sense of competition among their members, creating many competitors and few rewards.

# Ways to manage conflict within your team

**1 LISTEN CAREFULLY**
Find out what's on people's minds, and ask them what they're thinking and how they feel.

**2 SEPARATE PEOPLE FROM PROBLEMS**
Rather than saying "I can't support you", say "I'm not in favour of that solution."

**3 FOCUS ON INTERESTS**
Don't focus on a person's demands, but on their interests – the reasons behind their demands.

**4 RECOGNIZE FEELINGS**
Accept feelings in others, and work to communicate empathy. Keep your own emotions in check, to ensure that you act professionally.

**5 FIND THE SOURCE**
Track the conflict to its source. Don't accept the first answers you find; employees may have underlying concerns.

**6 KEEP COMMUNICATING**
Keep the lines of communication open and speak as frankly and honestly as possible.

**7 START SMALL**
Get people to agree on the small stuff first. Once they start to agree on a few things, the big issues won't be as difficult.

**8 DEVISE OPTIONS**
Find alternatives for mutual gain. By working together on the options, you can shift the dynamic from competition to cooperation.

**9 SUMMARIZE THE AGREEMENT**
Review all the details with everyone involved. Make sure all are in agreement.

**10 CUT YOUR LOSSES**
Sometimes the conflict has simply gone too far, and you must decide to make personnel changes.

# Chapter 4

# Communicating externally

In today's global economy, you may find yourself communicating across companies, countries, and cultures, through a variety of media, including the internet. Focus on your company's core goals and identity to ensure consistent messaging.

# Negotiating successfully

Negotiation is a process in which people attempt to persuade others to cooperate or assist in attaining goals or goods that they value. The process often involves bargaining – giving up something in order to get something else – as well as collaboration, cooperation, and compromise.

## Exploring interests

A key distinction to make in negotiating is recognizing the difference between interests and positions. A position is a hard line in the sand: a statement of a single acceptable outcome. Interests, on the other hand, are the reasons behind that position. Spend time seeing the negotiation from the other party's point of view; this may help you anticipate what is really important to them. This is important because there may be more than one way of meeting those interests. Can you find an alternative, workable position that will still satisfy the other party's interests?

# Recognizing significant points

Before negotiating, you need to decide upon three main points about your position:
• **Your target or aspiration point** What you hope to achieve. Set this at a high but reasonable level.
• **Your reservation or walk-away point** The least desirable outcome that you will accept. At anything less than your reservation, you would be better off walking away without a deal.
• **Your Best Alternative to a Negotiated Agreement (BATNA)** This is your back-up plan in case you are unable to reach agreement with the other party.

**TIP**

**CONSIDER COMPENSATION**

Sometimes parties can be enticed into an agreement through the offer of something unrelated to the issues in negotiation. Think about what might be valuable to the other party, but inexpensive for you to offer.

# Making the opening offer

If you have done your homework and have a good idea of the bargaining range, then you should make the opening offer. That offer anchors the bargaining process. Your opening offer should reflect your aspirations, but not be ridiculous. If it is way out of range, you risk insulting the other party and damaging trust. If the other party makes the opening offer, and it is outrageous, don't discuss it. Simply dismiss it, indicate that it is not a possibility, and start again.

Your opening offer should leave you room to make concessions, but bear in mind that any you do make will provide the other party with information. If they make concessions, you should reciprocate, or they may view you with distrust and become more competitive. Don't make too large a concession right away, however, or the other side may think there is considerable "give" in your bargaining range.

**? ASK YOURSELF...
AM I PREPARED
TO NEGOTIATE?**

• What do I really want?
• What does the other party involved really want?
• Should I compete, or should I cooperate with them?
• How honest should I be? Should I reveal all that I know?
• How much should I trust the people I'm negotiating with?

# Selling

Selling is both a form of persuasion and a process of relationship building. Most people don't want to feel as if they're being sold something; they would prefer to believe that they're buying it. This involves a balance of thoughtful questions, active listening, and a well-prepared presentation.

## Prospecting and presenting

Selling involves actively looking for prospects who have the money, the authority, and a desire to buy. Before you contact a prospect, make sure that they fulfil these criteria, and that you know both what you want to achieve, and how. Develop a presentation that you can deliver confidently. This may be entirely memorized, formulaic (allowing some buyer–seller interaction), or entirely flexible and interactive. If you're offering a solution to a specific problem, base your proposal around a detailed analysis of the buyer's situation. Before you contact a prospect, always:

• Determine your call objectives. Are they specific, measurable, achievable, realistic, and well-timed?
• Develop a customer profile. What do you know about the person who is making the buying decision?
• Familiarize yourself with all the customer benefits.
• Develop a sales presentation.

## Closing the sale

First ask the prospect's opinion about the benefits you're offering, using a question such as: "How does this sound to you?" If this throws up any objections, handle them as they arise. Don't repeat negative statements or concerns; focus on positive outcomes. There are various ways to close a sale, so choose the one that is most appropriate to your situation.

**TIP**

**MAKE A POSITIVE FIRST IMPRESSION**

Be positive: smile, be enthusiastic, and open conversation with a thoughtful compliment or a prediction related to your product.

**USE THE MINOR POINTS CLOSE**
Ask the prospect to make low-risk decisions on minor, low-cost elements. Then ask for the order.

## Ways to close a sale

**GIVE AN ALTERNATIVE CHOICE**
Give two options, and then ask: "Which of these do you prefer?"

**USE THE ASSUMPTIVE CLOSE**
When the prospect is close to a decision, say: "I'll call your order in tonight."

**SUMMARIZE THE BENEFITS**
Present the main features, advantages, and benefits, then ask for the order.

**USE THE SCARCITY CLOSE**
If true, tell the prospect that these items are so popular, there may not be many of them left.

**USE THE CONTINUOUS "YES" CLOSE**
Develop a set of questions the prospect will answer "yes" to, then ask for the order.

# Communicating across countries and cultures

The industrialized nations of the world are experiencing unprecedented change. In much of Europe, for example, it is possible for EU citizens to travel from country to country without a passport, conducting transactions in a common currency. Barriers to trade have tumbled or vanished in recent years, but through it all, each of us has retained something essential to our identity as humans: our culture.

## Defining culture

Culture is everything that people have, think, and do as members of their society. Culture affects and is a central part of our economy and the organizations that employ us. It is composed of material objects, ideas, values, and attitudes, as well as expected patterns of behaviour. Whatever your business, you're likely to encounter people of different ethnicity, citizenship, and cultural origin. Dealing with people of different cultures, conducting business over international borders, travelling safely, and communicating effectively are not always easy, but are essential for success in today's business world.

 **IN FOCUS... ETHNOCENTRISM**

All cultures, to one degree or another, display ethnocentrism: the tendency to evaluate a foreigner's behaviour by the standards of one's own culture, and to believe that one's culture is superior to all others. We tend to take our own culture for granted. We're born into it, and we live with its rules and assumptions day in and day out. We quickly come to believe that the way we live is simply "the way things should be". As a result, we often see our behaviour as correct. However, culture is not value-neutral. We have good reasons for believing and behaving as we do, but that doesn't necessarily mean that others are "wrong".

**INVESTIGATE THE SUBCULTURES**
Virtually all large, complex cultures contain subcultures. These are small groups of people with separate and specialized interests – essentially, they are niche markets.

# Understanding culture

When you're communicating with a culture other than your own, you need to be sensitive about the particular beliefs and values of that culture, and how they differ from your own. Bear in mind that:

• **Culture is ingrained** Few of us would give a moment's thought to learning how to be a part of the culture we have grown up in. Our first culture is so closely defined for each of us that we're barely aware that we have one. Learning a second culture, though, takes a purposeful effort.

• **Culture is universal** All societies have an interest in passing along values and norms to their children, thereby creating and defining a culture. No matter where you travel, you'll find people with cultures that differ from the one in which you grew up; noticing these differences will strengthen your communications.

• **Cultures allocate values** Some cultures engage in behaviours that others might consider reprehensible. Be careful never to cause offence when communicating by inadvertently breaking taboos or talking about matters that are considered "off limits".

# Recognizing change

The culture of any country is constantly undergoing change. The clothing people wear, the transportation they use, the books they read, the topics they talk about, and so on, all change over time. This is due to the internal forces of discovery, invention, and innovation; and external forces, including the diffusion of ideas from other cultures. Some cultures change fast, while others evolve more slowly, either by preference or because they are more physically isolated. Changes in culture are often reflected in changes in the way people speak and write; make sure that your own communications reflect these changes.

# Communicating internationally

On a personal level, communicating across international borders means becoming more aware of the ways in which your thinking or actions are culturally biased. Start by recognizing that your own education, background, and beliefs may be considered fine, or even laudable in your own culture, but they may not count for so much to someone from a different country. Take a non-judgemental position towards those from other cultures, and you are likely to find that they will extend the same hospitable tolerance towards you. If you find yourself making personal judgements, keep them to yourself.

When you're writing or speaking to people from another culture, try to understand life from their perspective. Learn to communicate respect for other people's ways, their country, and their values.

# Adopting the right attitude

You don't have to adopt the local culture and begin doing things the way they do. Just be aware and respect that they do things differently. "Your way" of communicating might work brilliantly in your own culture, but less well in another. Try to adopt an open-minded approach, focusing on:

• **Developing a tolerance for ambiguity** Accept the fact that you'll never understand everything about another culture. You can still appreciate and function within that culture satisfactorily.

• **Becoming more flexible** Things won't always go the way you want. A small measure of flexibility will prove enormously helpful.

• **Practising a little humility** Acknowledge what you do not know or understand. Because you weren't raised in another's culture (or may not even speak the language well), you'll never fully understand all aspects of it. Displaying humility and acceptance will win friends, influence people, and make life easier. Communication consists of the transfer of meaning, so do everything you can to make sure that your messages are not misunderstood.

**TIP**

**LEARN TO RECOGNIZE "NO"**

Some cultures consider it rude to say "no". If you are met with vague answers to requests, such as "I'll try", or "yes, but it may be difficult" in these cultures, it may be safer to assume that your request has been refused.

## ❓ ASK YOURSELF... **DO I UNDERSTAND THE CULTURE?**

• Do I understand the basic business etiquette of introductions and meetings in this new culture?
• Do I know how to recognize the key decision-makers within a group?
• Am I familiar with the culture's business dress code?
• Do I know how many languages are spoken, and which is the official language?
• Have I learned the preferred forms of negotiation?
• Do I know which forms of media are popular among which demographic groups?

# Writing for the web

The way that people read a website is very different to the way in which they read other written information. You must take this into account when developing content for a website. It is not sufficient to simply repurpose content written for print; you need to write specifically for the internet, thinking carefully about your audience and what they need.

## Engaging your readers

Why is writing for the internet different? First, people rarely read websites word-for-word. Instead, they scan the page, picking out individual words and sentences. Rather than starting at the beginning of a page and reading from start to finish, internet readers will scan a site looking for relevant items and then, if they find something useful, print it for later reference. Guide your reader by highlighting the most important or useful points in your document using headings, lists, and eye-catching typography.

**AVOID FRAGMENTATION**
Be careful not to subdivide your information into too many pieces. Your readers may be overwhelmed or frustrated if they have too many choices. Ensure that each segment is sensibly organized, coherent, and easy to scan.

Web readers generally do not read pages in sequence. Instead, they jump around on a website looking for content that interests them, navigating back and forth across images, ideas, and words. Providing information in precise segments or "chunks" will allow readers to quickly find what they're looking for. A well-constructed chunk provides readers with a comprehensive account, as well as links to related or supporting pages. When your content lends itself to such treatment, use lists rather than paragraphs. Readers can pick out information more easily from a list than from a fully developed paragraph.

## Preparing content for the web

**THINK ABOUT LENGTH**
Limit the length of each paragraph and each page to about half of what you might consider for a printed page. Don't arbitrarily divide a page that is likely to be printed.

**USE SUMMARIES**
Include brief but comprehensive summaries of longer documents, so that readers can easily tell whether they need to read more or can move on to other content.

**ENSURE EASY ACCESS**
Your principal goal should be to provide access to the information people are most likely to want. Provide easy-to-follow clues that will lead people to chunks of information that will be useful to them.

**PREPARE FOR PRINT**
Make it easy for your readers to find, print, and save information. If some aspects of your content are more detailed or lengthy, consider linking to a PDF file that is both downloadable and printable.

# Running a teleconference

Recent improvements in both the cost and quality of teleconferencing equipment have made the prospect of connecting people with audio and video technology over vast distances seem increasingly attractive. It is vital to plan carefully, however, to avoid technical hitches and make the experience rewarding and successful for those involved.

## Preparing for a teleconference

Running a successful and productive teleconference depends largely on the time you spend planning and preparing for it. If possible, find out as much as you can about the facility you have chosen before the day of the teleconference. If you're in charge, it is up to you to make sure that the setting has everything you need. Try to meet the support technician, and learn what your physical responsibilities will involve.

## CHAIRING A TELECONFERENCE

**FAST TRACK**

**OFF TRACK**

| FAST TRACK | OFF TRACK |
|---|---|
| Asking people to give their names, titles, and locations | Introducing some of the participants, but ignoring others |
| Keeping to the agenda and staying on time | Introducing new items not agreed to in advance |
| Taking control and providing people with opportunities to speak | Allowing people to talk with one another in side conversations |
| Making notes of what is being said and by whom | Failing to capture what's been said and agreed to |

# Appearing well

On the day, dress conservatively: avoid busy patterns, thin stripes, and small prints that draw attention. Act always as if people are watching you, and refrain from quirky mannerisms – these may go unnoticed in a meeting but are magnified in a teleconference. Sit up straight, pay attention, and project a professional image. Do your best to look at the camera lens when you are speaking. You'll enhance your credibility dramatically if you focus squarely on the camera; others will think you're speaking directly to them.

# Sounding good

Once you're in the room, avoid idle talk or unguarded comments – assume that someone may be watching and listening. Speak a bit more slowly than usual, to ensure that everyone understands you. Don't read a speech or a prepared statement, but keep summarizing key issues as you move along. Refer to the agenda and remind people of elapsed time as you move from point to point.

At the end of the teleconference, summarize the issues discussed and agreed to. After the event, prepare and distribute minutes within a few days.

## HOW TO... PLAN A TELECONFERENCE

Identify the purpose of the teleconference: explain to people what they will be doing and why.

↓

Visit the facility in advance and try to identify any aspects of the location or equipment that affect how you need to plan the teleconference.

↓

Identify a chairperson who will be responsible for starting, stopping, and running the teleconference.

↓

Plan the agenda; don't just try to "wing it" as you go along. Place easily accomplished items first on the list.

↓

Distribute the agenda so other people know what will be discussed and will have time to gather necessary information.

↓

Schedule the teleconference for a time and date that suits everyone.

↓

Confirm the teleconference with all participants and send a reminder just before it is due to take place.

↓

Share important resources in advance; send through any materials that are important for everyone to see.

# Communicating in a crisis

There is a huge difference between business problems and crises. Problems are commonplace in business. A crisis, on the other hand, is a major, unpredictable event. Without careful communication, crises have the potential to damage an organization's reputation and financial standing, together with those of its employees, shareholders, products, and services.

## Identifying the crisis

Some business crises can be prepared for (to a certain extent), while others require an immediate and creative response. There are two main types:
• **Internal crises** These arise within the company, such as accounting scandals, or labour strikes.
• **External crises** These are caused by an external factor, such as a natural disaster, a technological disaster, or external threats by special-interest groups.
   It is important to recognize the type of crisis you are facing, as this will help you pinpoint the groups of people you will need to communicate with, and give you an idea of how fast and how far the effects of the crisis could potentially spread.

## CASE STUDY

### Merck & Company

In September 2004, pharmaceutical firm Merck & Company made the decision to remove its painkilling drug Vioxx from the market because of cardiovascular risks. More than 100 million prescriptions had been written for the drug. Within 60 hours of the initial announcement, Merck's communications team launched a website and established a toll-free telephone number to address concerns.

Traffic on the company's Vioxx website grew from 4,000 hits daily to 234,000 in just 24 hours. The toll-free number received more than 120,000 calls in the first six days following the announcement. Without its sophisticated web presence and competently staffed call centre, Merck would not have been able to address the enormous wave of public concern that arose overnight about Vioxx, and its reputation would have been badly damaged.

# Dealing with a crisis

Communicating in a crisis is different from managing a business problem. You are likely to be unprepared, and have insufficient information. This is accompanied by intense time pressure and an escalating flow of events. Crisis communication often offers few precedents to work from and intense scrutiny from outside the organization. This can lead to a loss of control and a sense of panic, so it is important to keep your head, and address the crisis systematically.

## ADDRESSING A CRISIS

| WHAT TO DO | HOW TO DO IT |
| --- | --- |
| Get information | • Deal from an informed position and separate fact from rumour. Document what you know and don't know for sure. Become the source of reliable information, and keep the information flowing.<br>• Determine the real problem in the short term and the long term. Check whether this is really your problem. |
| Put people in place | • Put someone in charge. Give them responsibility, authority, and the resources to get the job done. Tell people who it is.<br>• Assemble an effective but nimble team. Staff it with the expertise needed, and provide resources. Isolate team members from other day-to-day concerns. |
| Draw up a plan | • Develop a strategy, which should include ways to resolve the problem, deal with affected parties, and communicate both today and in the long term.<br>• Establish goals. Define your objectives for the short term, mid-term, and long term. Measure relentlessly and don't be discouraged by critics, negative press, or short-term failures. |
| Start communicating | • Centralize communications. Incoming communication provides intelligence, while outgoing communication gives a measure of control over what is being said about the situation.<br>• Rely on a strictly limited number of spokespersons who are knowledgeable, authoritative, responsive, patient, and good humoured.<br>• Consider all markets – local, regional, national, and international. Don't overlook allies in other markets who may be able to provide assistance or credibility. |

# Dealing with the media

Being the subject of a news media interview is never easy, and can be stressful and risky. You might say the wrong thing or forget to say what's most important about the subject of the interview, or your comments might be taken out context when they're aired. However, by following a few basic rules, you can limit risk and use the interview to your advantage.

**TIP**

**REVIEW THE DAY'S NEWS**

Make sure you're up to date on events surrounding the topic of the interview. If you're caught by surprise, don't comment on events or quotes on which you are uncertain.

## Capitalizing on opportunity

Learn to see media interviews as an opportunity to reach a large audience. They represent a chance to tell your story and to inform the public of your business or expertise. They also offer an opportunity to address public concerns and set the record straight, if you're the subject of misinformation in the press. They can be a forum in which to apologize if you've done something wrong, and a chance to reinforce the credibility of your organization and its leadership. Don't feel bullied into giving an interview if you're not ready: you can say "no" or delegate to another staff member who is more accustomed to dealing with the media.

### ✔ CHECKLIST SUCCEEDING IN MEDIA INTERVIEWS

|  | YES | NO |
|---|---|---|
| • Are you clear about what you hope to achieve from the interview? | ☐ | ☐ |
| • Do you know which items of information you can share, and which are confidential? | ☐ | ☐ |
| • Have you decided on a method for avoiding arguments if the reporter goads you? | ☐ | ☐ |
| • Do you know how to respond to false allegations, without repeating the phrases the reporter uses? | ☐ | ☐ |
| • Are you focused on remaining professional and likeable, no matter what happens in the interview? | ☐ | ☐ |

# Preparing for an interview

The best way to ensure a good interview is thorough preparation. Gather your information, and also:
• Research the reporter; deal only with established, professional journalists.
• Ask your Public Affairs or Corporate Communication office for help and guidance.
• Find out the subject and background of the story and ask who else is participating.
• Double-check the time, date, and location.
• Refine and practise your message: rehearse aloud the words you actually plan to use.

**TIP**

**GET YOUR POINT IN EARLY**

A reporter may not ask the one question you're most hoping to talk about. Raise the issue yourself, get your points in, and repeat them frequently. Use the free air time or print space to your benefit.

# Conducting the interview

Arrive at the appointed interview site early and introduce yourself to all those involved. Dress smartly and accept the offer of make-up if appropriate: knowing that you look good will add to your confidence and sense of professionalism.

During the interview, it's perfectly acceptable to refer to facts and figures on a pocket card. Be yourself, and use words that everyone will understand; explain any technical or complex concepts in simple ways, as though you're talking to a friend. Make sure that you stay focused on the central theme of your message and always speak in terms of the public's interest, not your own.

# Building brands

Communicating the essence of a brand is more than simply using words and visuals to convey an image. This is because a brand is both a process and a product. It's a living, breathing organism that must be nurtured and protected if it is to survive and thrive.

## HOW TO... BUILD A BRAND

First, deliver something of value.

↓

Then, meet expectations every day.

↓

Be clear and certain about who you are.

↓

Represent the same thing to every customer.

## Winning hearts and minds

A brand is, first of all, a promise of an experience. It is what a product, service, or company stands for in the minds of customers and prospects. At its very core, a brand is a perception or a feeling. It's the feeling evoked when we think about a product or the company that delivers it. And, of course, a brand is the basis for differentiation in the marketplace – a way to separate yourself from all other competitors in the hearts and minds of your customers.

## Defining the brand

The most crucial characteristics of a brand are content and consistency. To succeed, a brand must make a clear and unambiguous promise to its stakeholders (customers, employees, investors, suppliers, creditors, and others) and then deliver on that promise.

The Starbucks brand, for example, is clearly aligned with the customer experience. When regulars in Starbucks' coffee shops began to complain about the smell of hot breakfast sandwiches, the company's CEO Howard Schultz decided to focus on the core experience (and aromas) of freshly ground coffee, and the relaxing experience of visiting a Starbucks. Retail giant Wal-Mart's brand promise is "Everyday low prices". It makes no promises about customer service, brand-name products, or the shopping experience.

# Communicating brand image

There are five key points to consider when defining and maintaining a successful brand:

• **Vision** Be certain that one consistent, strategic vision drives your goals for the brand. Prioritize your plan to deliver on the promise (what is most important and why?). Align all stakeholders behind the vision.

• **Culture** Empower your entire organization to get behind the brand. Give them the authority, responsibility, resources, and training to satisfy customer expectations.

• **Innovation** You cannot stand still; you must continually innovate to stay ahead of the demands of the marketplace and the shifts in everything from demographics to target-group tastes and preferences. Demonstrate that you are both innovative and protective of the brand experience.

• **Action** Specify and communicate those actions that are essential to brand success to those within the organization who must deliver on the promise.

• **Value** Consistently and continually measure results. Show your investors, associates, and business partners what you've accomplished and what improvements you have yet to make.

**TIP**

**LOOK TO YOUR CUSTOMERS**

If you feel your brand needs updating, turn to your customer research. What is it they seek in your brand? What do they value the most? And what changes will they accept?

## IN FOCUS... BRAND VALUE

Brands that have a clear sense of themselves and have worked diligently to deliver on their promises are often quite durable, withstanding economic down-turns, changes in customer preferences, and game-changing innovations in their product category. The value of developing brands is highlighted in two quotes. John Stuart, former CEO of Quaker Oats Company, said: "If this company were split up, I would gladly give you the property, plant, and equipment, and I would take the brands and trademarks… and I would fare better than you." Carlton Curtis, VP of Corporate Communication at Coca-Cola, stated: "If all of Coca-Cola's assets were destroyed overnight, whoever owned the Coca-Cola name could walk into a bank the next morning and get a loan to rebuild everything."

# Index

# Acknowledgements

### Author's acknowledgements
My thanks to the good people at cobalt id who have helped me condense decades of experience, teaching, and research into an interesting, readable volume. Had Marek Walisiewicz not called and asked me to consider this project, I'd never have gotten it done. My appreciation goes, in particular, to Kati Dye and the other talented artists, editors, and designers who've transformed my thoughts and observations into a lovely book. My thanks, as well, to Daniel Mills and the very professional staff of Dorling Kindersley whose diligence and professionalism with this title and this series have been nothing short of remarkable. Thanks to you all.

### Dedication
To Pam, Colleen, Molly, and Kathleen. And to Jay, Cianan, and Ty. Your inspiration, patience, and support have been indispensable. Thank you for making this possible.

To my Notre Dame colleagues: Sandra, Cynthia, and Sondra. You are among the many who have encouraged me, corrected me, kept me honest, and held me accountable for my ideas. And to Andrea: teaching and writing are so much easier with your help.

And, of course, to my friends in the Management Communication Association and the Arthur W. Page Society. Thank you for the support, counsel, and good ideas. My life is richer for having shared your company.

### Publisher's acknowledgements
The publisher would like to thank Hilary Bird for indexing, Judy Barratt for proofreading, and Charles Wills for co-ordinating Americanization.

### Picture credits
The publisher would like to thank the following for their kind permission to reproduce their photographs:

1 Alamy: Herbert Kehrer/imagebroker; 4–5 Alamy: artpartner-images.com; 8–9 Getty Images: Justin Pumfrey; 11 iStockphoto.com: Eric Isselée/Global Photographers; 13 iStockphoto.com: PeterNunes_Photography; 19 iStockphoto.com: Guillermo Perales Gonzalez; 22–23 (background) Alamy: Dan Atkin; 22–23 (sticky notes) iStockphoto.com: Julien Grondin; 28–29 iStockphoto.com: Kevin Russ; 32–33 iStockphoto.com: Robert Kohlhuber; 34 iStockphoto.com: blackred; 44–45 Alamy: David Osborn; 51 Getty Images: Darrin Klimek; 55 Getty Images: David Gould; 58 iStockphoto.com: Hanquan Chen; 60–61 iStockphoto.com: Susan Trigg; 67 Getty Images: Peter Dazeley.

Every effort has been made to trace the copyright holders. The publisher apologizes for any unintentional omission and would be pleased, in such cases, to place an acknowledgement in future editions of this book.